JAN LADISLAV DUSSEK
SIX SONATINAS
Op.19
Edited by Lionel Salter

THE ASSOCIATED BOARD OF
THE ROYAL SCHOOLS OF MUSIC

INTRODUCTION

Jan Ladislav Dussek's life-story was an adventurous one. Born in 1760 in a small Bohemian town 70 miles east of Prague, he studied in his native country, but at the age of 19 was taken by a patron to Malines, where he taught the piano. Thence in rapid succession he went to Berg-op-Zoom as organist of one of its principal churches; to Amsterdam, where his playing created a sensation; and to The Hague, where he gave lessons to the children of the Stadtholder. In 1782 he was in Hamburg, receiving some instruction from C.P.E.Bach; and the following year he played before Catherine the Great in St.Petersburg before going to Lithuania for a couple of years as *Kapellmeister* to Prince Karl Radziwill. He then made an extended tour of Germany as a virtuoso on the piano and the glass harmonica before staying for two years in Paris, where Marie Antoinette became his enthusiastic admirer. On the outbreak of the Revolution, Dussek fled to London, where he spent some 11 years as a fashionable piano teacher and married the singer and harpist Sophia Corri. He performed frequently at Salomon's concerts, appeared with Haydn (who praised his 'remarkable talents'), encouraged the piano manufacturer Broadwood to extend the instrument's range to six octaves, and set up a music publishing business with his father-in-law. When this collapsed, however, Dussek left Corri in the lurch and fled to Hamburg, where he gave concerts (at which he was apparently the first to place the piano sideways on the platform) before moving back to his native Bohemia. He then entered the service first of Prince Louis Ferdinand of Prussia (where their rackety life was described by Spohr in his autobiography) and later of Talleyrand in Paris. There, after giving numerous concerts where his playing had 'a magic of performance, a power and a charm of expression which were truly irresistible', he died of gout in 1812.

The present six sonatinas, listed both as Op.19 and Op.20, were originally 'pour le Fortepiano ou le Clavecin avec Accompagnement d'une Flutte', as the 1792 edition printed by Longman and Broderip has it; but they then re-emerged as piano solos. Unfortunately that original contains very many obvious errors and inconsistencies, which the present edition, while remaining as faithful as possible to Dussek's text, has endeavoured to correct. Dynamic markings, occurring erratically in the early publication, have been placed more rationally and somewhat increased in number; phrasing and articulation, fingering and metronome marks are editorial.

LIONEL SALTER
London, 1983

Sonatina in G

DUSSEK, Op.19 No.1

RONDO
Allegretto: Tempo di Minuetto [♪ = 120]

Sonatina in C

Op.19 No.2

Allegretto quasi Andante [♩ = 104]

RONDO
Non presto [♩ = 116]

Da Capo al ⊕ *poi alla Coda*

CODA

Sonatina in F

Op.19 No.3

RONDO
Andantino [♪ = 100]

Da Capo al ✛ poi alla Coda **CODA**

Sonatina in A

Op.19 No.4

MINUETTO
Tempo di ballo [♩ = 104]

Sonatina in C

Op.19 No.5

RONDO
Allegretto moderato [♩ = 100]

FINE

Dal Segno 𝄋 al Fine

Sonatina in E flat

Op.19 No.6

RONDO
Allegretto [♩. = 76]

CODA

Processed and printed by
Halstan & Co. Ltd., Amersham, Bucks., England